snapshot•picture•library

BUGS

snapshot · picture · library

BUGS

FOG CITY PRESS

Published by Fog City Press,
a division of Weldon Owen Inc.
415 Jackson Street
San Francisco, CA 94111 USA
www.weldonowen.com

WELDON OWEN INC.
Group Publisher, Bonnier Publishing Group John Owen
Chief Executive Officer and President Terry Newell
Senior Vice President, International Sales Stuart Laurence
Vice President, Sales and New Business Development Amy Kaneko
Vice President, Publisher Roger Shaw
Vice President, Creative Director Gaye Allen
Managing Editor, Fog City Press Karen Perez
Assistant Editor Sonia Vallabh
Art Director Bret Hansen
Designer Andreas Schueller
Design Assistant Kevin Yuen
Production Director Chris Hemesath
Production Manager Michelle Duggan
Color Manager Teri Bell

Text Sonia Vallabh
Picture Research Brandi Valenza

A WELDON OWEN PRODUCTION
© 2008 Weldon Owen Inc.

Library of Congress Control Number: 2008926993

ISBN-13: 978-1-74089-992-5

10 9 8 7 6 5 4 3 2 1
2009 2010 2011 2012

Printed by Tien Wah Press in Singapore.

Did you know that more than
half of all known creatures
are bugs? They may not
be very big, but bugs have
strength in numbers. They
are the most diverse group
of animals on Earth!

Whether they're long or
short, smooth or spiky,
gliding through the air
or hiding underground,
bugs are everywhere.
And that means that anyone
can go exploring for bugs...
So what are you waiting for?

Not all bugs are creepy-crawly. Many are beautiful and bright.

Some, like these butterflies,
are covered in pretty patterns
and stripes.

Beetles are often shiny, and come in all of the colors of the rainbow.

These bugs all
share one thing:
polka-dots!

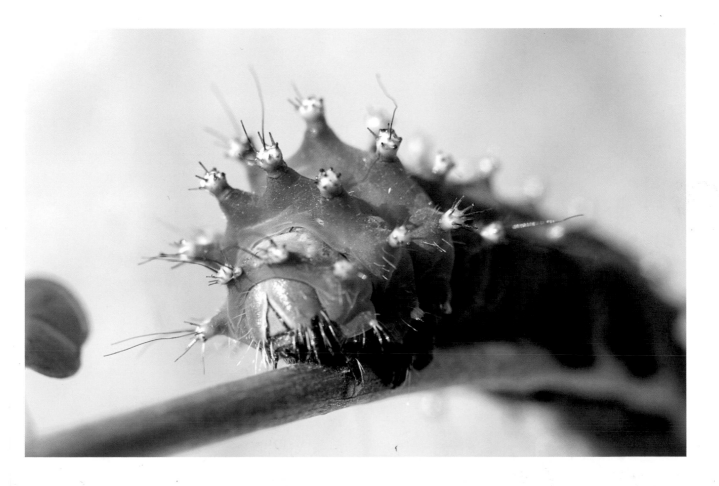

Bright colors can
be a warning to
other animals. This
ladybug's bright
red color says that
it's not good to eat.

On some bugs, stripes are useful for hiding. On other bugs, bright stripes are a warning to other animals to stay away.

This snail may look slow and harmless, but snails can be bad for the garden because they like to eat the fresh green leaves of our plants.

Bugs come in thousands of wacky shapes and sizes.

Some insects, like this spiny flower mantis, hide by making themselves look like something else: what a pretty flower this bug makes!

Other bugs
blend in so well
that they can
hardly be seen!
Can you see the
moth below?

It's easy to see
a busy group
of bugs.

And large bugs
like the stag beetle,
which can be as big
as your hand, are
hard not to notice!

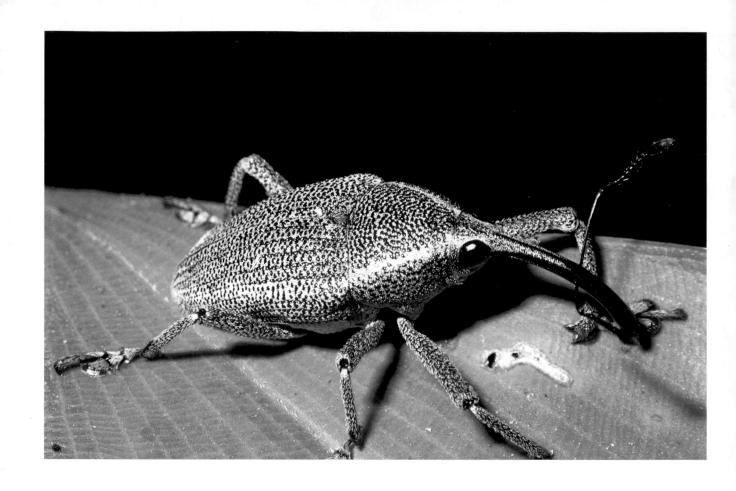

Some bugs have long snouts for eating. Others have big jaws for fighting.

Some insects look
like they have
thick, furry coats!

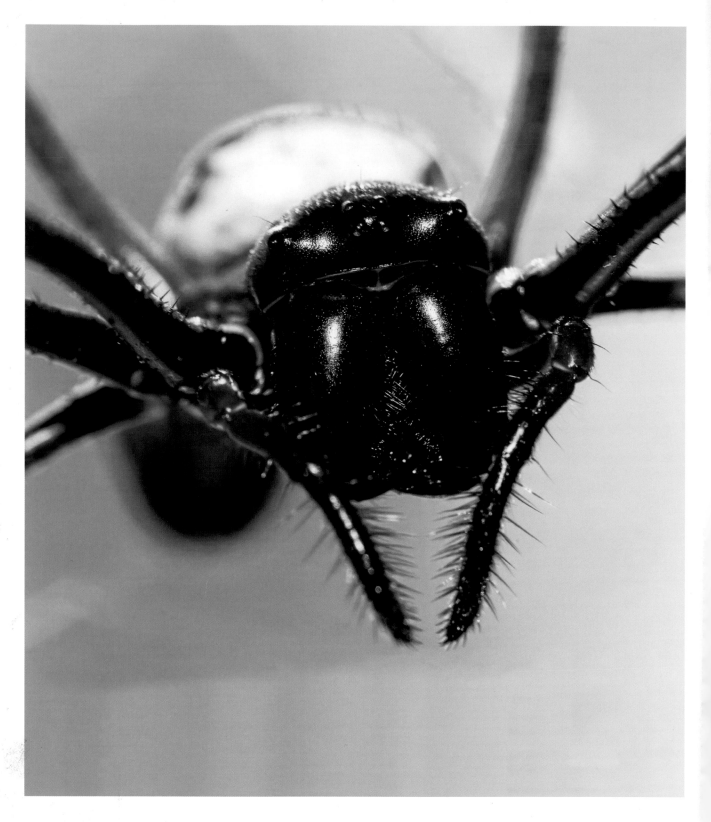

Many bugs have compound eyes, which is like having thousands of eyes in one. This allows them to see in almost every direction.

Yellow bear caterpillars cannot see much because their eyes are so small. They must move their front ends back and forth to feel where to go next!

Bugs can change a lot as they grow up. Baby bugs are called larvae or nymphs.

As adults, bugs may look completely different. What a surprise!

Bugs can often be
found on brightly
colored flowers.

Flowers offer
these bugs food,
and in return,
the bugs spread
the flowers'
pollen as they
move from
place to place.

Bugs use their fancy feelers, or antennae, to find the foods that they like to eat.

Caterpillars
spend almost all
day munching
on plants.

Honeybees have a special talent.
They make a food that we like
to harvest and eat—honey! Yum!

This wolf spider looks like it has a different kind of food in mind— probably another bug! Wolf spiders run after their prey.

Other spiders build traps to catch
their dinner unawares.

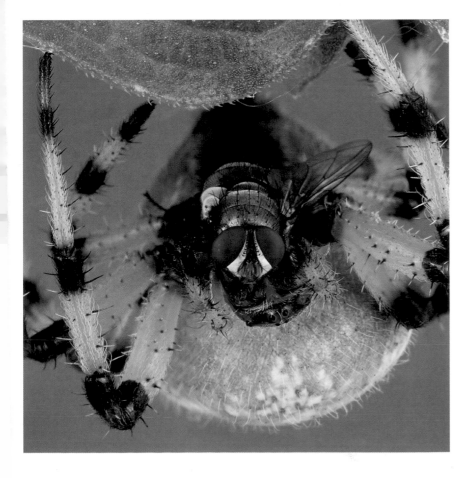

I wouldn't want to be a little bug when a big bug is hungry.

You just never
know who you'll
meet next in the
bug world!

Widow Skimmer Dragonfly

 Ladybug

 Tobacco Hornworm Moth

 Assassin Bug

 Stink Bug

 Jamaican Field Cricket

 Black Swallowtail Butterfly Caterpillar

 Colorado Potato Beetle

 Green June Beetles

 Blue Morpho Butterfly

 Dung Beetle

 Fireflies

 Swallowtail Butterfly

 Garden Snail

 Red Ants

 Butterfly

 Wheel Bug

 Stag Beetle

 Rose Chafer

 Caterpillar

 Long Snout Weevil

 Spotted Cucumber Beetle

 Grasshoppers

 Stag Beetle

 Colorado Beetle Larva

 Spiny Flower Mantis

 Snout Beetle

 Giant Peacock Moth Caterpillar

Green Shield Bug

June Beetle

Orb Spider

 Julia Butterfly

 Wolf Spider

 Grasshopper

 Nais Metalmark Butterfly

 Cross Spider

 Yellow Bear Caterpillar

 Bee

 Baboon Spider

 Henry's Marsh Moth Caterpillar

 Ladybug

 Green Shield Bug and Spider

 Beet Armyworm Larva

 Violet Tanbark Beetle

 Banana Spider

 Swallowtail Caterpillar

 Beetle

 Shamrock Spider

 Butterfly

 Swallowtail Caterpillar

 Mantis

 Butterfly

 Honeybees

 Grasshopper

Common Banner Butterflies

 Bumblebee

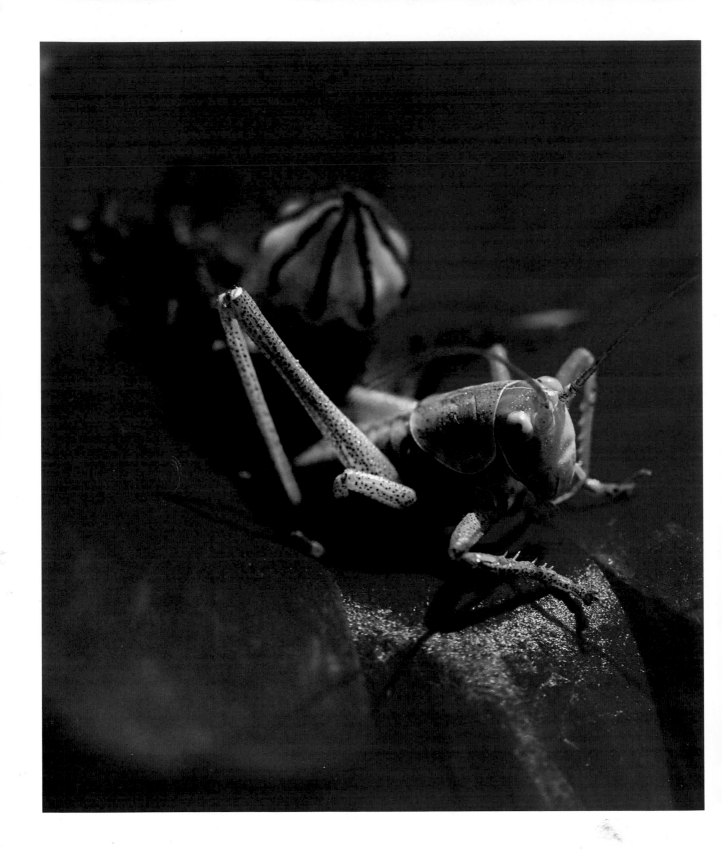

ACKNOWLEDGMENTS

Weldon Owen would like to thank the following people for their assistance in the production of this book: Diana Heom, Ashley Martinez, Danielle Parker, Lucie Parker, Phil Paulick, and Erin Zaunbrecher.

CREDITS

All images courtesy of Shutterstock.